2

Copycat Recipes

A Complete Cookbook for Duplicating Your Favorite

Restaurant Foods at Home

Nicole Shaker

original author of this work can be in any fashion deemed liable for any hardship or damages that may befall them after undertaking information described herein.

Additionally, the information in the following pages is intended only for informational purposes and should thus be thought of as universal. As befitting its nature, it is presented without assurance regarding its prolonged validity or interim quality. Trademarks that are mentioned are done without written consent and can in no way be considered an endorsement from the trademark holder.

Table of Contents

Introduction

I would like to thank you and congratulate you for getting this book, Copycat Recipes.

Food is functional to life, but life is happiness and joy, it is the pursuit of pleasure and its constant experimentation.

Consuming the foods, we enjoy can lift our spirits and make us feel satisfied and relaxed.

On the other hand, consuming our favorite foods can sometimes cause negative effects such as guilt and remorse.

How can we minimize the negative impacts that food has on our mood and maximize the positive ones?

You don't have to be a master chef to prepare these dishes.

In this Copycat Recipes book, you will realize that you can cook those expensive and delicious restaurant dishes at home, in your own kitchen, with materials and products easily available in the market and grocery stores without spending a penny more.

You can modify the dishes according to your taste and dietary guidelines.

You will have the freedom of complete control over what is in your food, whether you put together fresh or packaged produce.

This can make all the difference in your overall health.

Another advantage of this Copycat Recipes book it gives you a chance to reconnect.

Cooking together can give you a chance to reconnect with your partner and your loved ones. Cooking also has other benefits. The American Psychological Association says that working together with new things" like learning a new recipe", can help maintain a relationship between a pair.

Cooking at home gives you the ability to enjoy the food you want, the way you like it, and you can also control portion sizes and, in a way, control food waste.

Cooking at home gives you a break from your routine and room for imagination. Plus, by following a duplicate recipe, you'll be able to serve an unforgettable meal.

With constant practice and experimentation, your cooking will be loved by family and friends. You will see them enjoying the best nutritious food because of you and your faith in spreading health and love.

Enjoy it!

Chapter 1: Appetizer Recipes

1. Chili's Boneless Buffalo Wings

Preparation time: 35 minutes

Servings: 2 to 4

Difficulty: Moderate

Ingredients:

- One cup of all-purpose flour
- Two teaspoons of salt
- Half teaspoon black pepper
- ¼ teaspoon cayenne pepper
- ¼ teaspoon paprika
- One egg, beaten
- One cup of milk
- Two boneless, skinless chicken breasts, each sliced into six pieces
- Four to six cups of vegetable oil
- One tablespoon of butter or margarine
- ¼ cup Crystal or Frank's hot sauce

For Serving

- Celery sticks
- Blue cheese dressing, homemade or store-bought

Instructions:

1. Combine the flour and dry seasonings in a medium bowl and whisk until well mixed. Whisk the egg and the milk together individually.

2. In the egg mixture, dip each chicken piece, shake it a little, then dip it in the flour mixture. On a baking sheet, lay the bits and refrigerate for 15 minutes.

3. Heat four cups of vegetable oil to 375 ° F in a large skillet. To fry the chicken, keep extra oil handy in case you need more.

4. Melt the butter and add the hot sauce; place it in a big bowl to set aside.

5. Fry the chicken pieces in batches until golden brown and fried (no longer pink in the middle). Drain on towels made of cloth. Place it in the butter-hot sauce mixture when all the chicken is fried, and toss.

6. Serve it on the side with celery sticks and blue cheese dressing.

2. Emeril's New Orleans's Rosemary Biscuits

Preparation time: 25 minutes

Servings: 12 biscuits

Difficulty: Easy

Ingredients:

- One cup of all-purpose flour, plus extra for dusting
- One teaspoon of baking powder
- Half a teaspoon of salt
- 1/8 teaspoon baking soda
- Three tablespoons of cold unsalted butter, cut into small pieces
- One tablespoon of minced fresh rosemary or One teaspoon of dried
- Half to 3/4 cup buttermilk

Instructions:

1. Preheat the oven to 450°F.
2. Mix the dry ingredients in a large bowl and whisk to blend thoroughly. Using a cookie cutter or two dinner knives to slice through the butter until the mixture resembles coarse crumbs. Add the rosemary, which is minced.
3. Drop about half a cup of buttermilk and carefully stir until the dough is just combined with a wooden spoon. Do not overmix since this would make the biscuits stiff.

4. Add a little more buttermilk if the dough appears too stiff. Shape it softly into a dough ball.

5. Flour a work surface like a cutting board and pat the dough ball out to a width of around 7 inches and a half-inch thick circle. Break the biscuits and put them on a baking sheet using a 1-inch diameter cookie cutter.

6. In between the biscuits, make sure to leave plenty of space.

7. Bake for 10 to 12 minutes, until the biscuits are lightly golden brown on the top and the sides. Serve it warm.

3. Hard Rock Café's Tupelo-style Chicken

Preparation time: 50 minutes

Servings: 6 to 8

Difficulty: Moderate

Ingredients:

- Honey-Mustard Dipping Sauce
- 1⁄4 cup mayonnaise
- One and a half teaspoons of yellow mustard
- Two teaspoons of honey
- Pinch of paprika
- Apricot Dipping Sauce
- Two tablespoons of Grey Poupon Dijon mustard
- One tablespoon of apricot preserves
- Two tablespoons of honey
- One cup of crumbled cornflakes
- Two teaspoons of red pepper flakes
- One and a quarter teaspoons of cayenne pepper
- One teaspoon of cumin
- One teaspoon of salt
- Half teaspoon of paprika
- A quarter teaspoon onion powder
- Pinch of garlic powder
- Four to six cups of vegetable oil for deep-frying
- One cup of milk

- One large egg, beaten
- One cup of all-purpose flour
- One pound of boneless, skinless chicken breasts

Instructions:

1. Make the sauce of honey-mustard. Whisk all of the ingredients together. Set aside in a fridge sealed until ready to use.

2. Create the apricot sauce by whisking together all of the ingredients. Set aside or, when ready to use, refrigerate, sealed.

3. Combine the cornflakes with the red pepper flakes, cayenne, cumin, cinnamon, paprika, onion powder, and garlic powder to make the bread. Whisk until it is well combined with the ingredients. Set in a shallow dish.

4. In a deep-fryer or a heavy-bottomed saucepan, preheat the oil to 350°F.

5. Whisk the milk and the egg together and put them in a shallow bowl. Put it in a shallow dish with the flour.

6. Split the chicken breasts into strips that are ½-inch wide. Cover in flour and the egg with each strip, then coat it again and coat the egg again. Press each strip into the cornflake mixture and fry it carefully, in lots, for 4 to 5 minutes before each strip is browned and fried through. Drain on towels made of cloth.

7. Serve with the two-hand ramekin dipping sauces.

4. Olive Garden's Clam Bruschetta

Preparation time: 35 minutes

Servings: 4

Difficulty: Moderate

Ingredients:

- Eight thick diagonally cut slices of Italian or French bread
- One clove garlic, cut in half
- Four large tomatoes, cut into eight thick slices
- One cup of chopped canned clam meat, drained
- Kosher salt
- Black pepper
- Half cup extra virgin olive oil
- 12 fresh basil leaves, shredded

Instructions:

1. Preheat the broiler or grill.

2. From both sides, toast the slices of bread. Rub the garlic with the split side of it.

3. On each slice of toasted bread, place one tomato slice and two tablespoons of clam meat and arrange the slices on a warmed serving tray. Sprinkle with salt and a few black pepper bits.

4. Sprinkle with olive oil and apply fresh basil to the top. Serve it warm.

5. Bennigan's Broccoli Bites

Preparation time: 40 minutes

Servings: 4

Difficulty: Easy

Ingredients:

Broccoli Bites

- Two cups of frozen chopped broccoli
- Three eggs
- 3⁄4 cup shredded Colby cheese
- 3⁄4 cup shredded Monterey jack cheese
- Five tablespoons of real bacon bits
- One tablespoon of diced yellow onion
- Two tablespoons of flour
- Four cups of oil for frying
- Italian breadcrumbs, as needed

Honey-Mustard Dipping Sauce

- 3⁄4 cup sour cream
- 1/3 cup mayonnaise
- 1/3 cup Dijon mustard
- 1/3 cup honey
- Four teaspoons of lemon juice

Instructions:

1. Thaw and properly drain the broccoli by squeezing it into a strainer. Using a whisk to beat the eggs in a mixing bowl until well mixed.

2. In a plastic container, put the broccoli, eggs, cheese, bacon bits, onion, and flour. Stir together until completely mixed with a spatula.

3. Refrigerate the mixture for 1 hour or so. This will aid in binding the blend, making preparing even easier.

4. In a fryer or deep pan, heat about 4 cups of oil at 350 °F. In a shallow pan, put the bread crumbs. Scoop in the bread crumbs for one tablespoon of a part of the broccoli mixture. Shape each part into a ball and cover it in the bread crumbs well.

5. Place the bites of broccoli in the frying basket or frying pan. Let aware they're not going to stay together. Fry for a minute.

6. Remove and place the excess oil on a plate lined with paper towels to absorb it.

7. Combine the sour cream, mayonnaise and mustard for the dipping sauce. Using a whisk, mix thoroughly. Pour the honey and lemon juice in slowly and blend until it is smooth and well mixed.

8. Serve with broccoli bites.

6. Morton's Steakhouse Shrimp Alexander

Preparation time: 35 minutes

Servings: 4

Difficulty: Moderate

Ingredients:

Breaded Shrimp

- Four ounces melted butter
- One pound of jumbo shrimp (8-12) to the pound
- One cup of plain breadcrumbs
- Three teaspoons of finely minced shallots
- Two teaspoons of finely chopped parsley
- One and a half tablespoons of finely chopped fresh garlic
- salt and pepper to taste

Beurre Blanc Sauce

- Three tablespoons of finely minced shallots
- Half cup of dry white wine inexpensive chardonnay is fine
- One to Two tablespoons of lemon juice
- Eight ounces unsalted butter
- A quarter teaspoon of salt

Instructions:

For Shrimp

1. Preheat the oven to 500 F.

2. Put the breadcrumbs, shallots, parsley and garlic together. To taste, you might want to add some salt and pepper.

3. Shell, devein and butterfly the shrimp

4. Dip the shrimp in butter (butter should be soft, not hot), then in a mixture of breadcrumbs, put the shrimp on the side of a small pan. Pour the excess butter into the pan so that the butter will cook the shrimp.

5. Beurre Blanc

6. In a shallow pan, mix the champagne, lemon juice, and shallots. Heat over moderate flame.

7. Reduce the heat to the lowest setting on your burner until the wine has decreased to just a tablespoon. Start applying butter to the small nobs, constantly stirring until the butter melts.

8. Continuously stir the sauce, adding more butter just after the last addition has melted and thickened the sauce.

9. When the sauce has thickened and is pale yellow, the sauce is full. Do not allow it to get too hot for the sauce, or it will split.

Chapter 2: Soup Recipes

1. Huston's Canadian Cheese Soup

Preparation time: 55 minutes

Servings: 4 to 6

Difficulty: Moderate

Ingredients:

- Eight tablespoons of (one stick) butter or margarine
- One cup of finely diced carrots
- Half cup finely diced onion
- Half cup finely diced celery
- Two to Three tablespoons of all-purpose flour
- Three cups of half-and-half
- Three cups of chicken broth
- Two pounds Velveeta cheese, cut into cubes

Garnish

- One tablespoon of minced fresh parsley
- Diced tomatoes
- Diced jalapeño pepper

Instructions:

1. Heat the butter in a large saucepan and sauté the carrots, onion, and celery. Do not brown the vegetables; they are only meant to be fluffy. Whisk and mix in the flour for a

---

minute or two, then add the half-and-a-half and boil over low heat. Don't let the mixture boil; once it is thickened, just let it simmer.

2. Add the chicken broth steadily, whisking up the mix to combine all the ingredients. Like a cream sauce, the broth can be slightly thickened. For around 10 minutes, let it boil, so the flour has a chance to cook.

3. Stir in the cheese until it is fully molten, continuously whisking. Garnish with the parsley and, if you prefer, the tomatoes and jalapeños with the soup in warmed cups.

2. Olive Garden's Italian Sausage Soup

Preparation time: 40 minutes

Servings: 4

Difficulty: Moderate

Ingredients:

- One pound of bulk sweet Italian sausage
- One cup of converted white rice
- Six cups of beef broth
- One cup of chopped tomatoes
- Two tablespoons of tomato paste
- Salt and pepper
- One 10-ounce box of frozen spinach, thawed, drained, and chopped
- Grated Pecorino Romano cheese for garnish

Instructions:

1. In a stockpot, sauté the sausage, breaking it up as it cooks. Add the rice until deeply browned and stir until it is completely covered in the sausage's fat. Bring to a boil, add beef broth, tomatoes, tomato paste, salt and 1/4 teaspoon of pepper.

2. Reduce the heat and simmer until the rice is tender, for 12 to 15 minutes. However, add the diced spinach to ensure that it is well-drained; if possible, squeeze it into

a dish towel to keep the moisture out. For a few minutes, let the soup boil, then season with salt and pepper.

3. Add the soup too hot bowls and garnish with the brushed cheese.

3. MGM Grand Spicy Jambalaya

Preparation time: 56 minutes

Servings: 6

Difficulty: Moderate

Ingredients:

- Six bay leaves
- pounds diced ham
- Two gallons of water
- vegetable oil for sauteing
- Five pounds diced chicken breast
- Two pounds chopped onions
- Two pounds chopped onions
- One and a half pounds chopped green pepper
- One cup of chopped green onions
- Two pounds diced tomatoes
- Two cups of tomato paste
- Three tablespoons of chopped parsley
- Four ounces chopped garlic
- Two teaspoons of dried thyme
- Two teaspoons of cayenne pepper
- A quarter cup Worcestershire sauce
- Three pounds smoked sausage
- Three pounds of rice
- One tablespoon of salt

Instructions

1. Add the bay leaves, chopped ham, and water to the boiler. Let boil for 1 hour.

2. Heat the oil in another pan. Add the diced chicken, celery and onions. Sauté and add the peppers, onions and diced tomatoes until tender.

3. Put in the tomato paste, chopped parsley, crushed garlic, dried thyme, Worcestershire sauce, cayenne pepper, and smoked sausage.

4. Fill the jambalaya with fried rice and add salt to taste.

4. Brennan's Onion Soup

Preparation time: 35 minutes

Servings: 8

Difficulty: Moderate

Ingredients:

- One and a half cups of butter
- Four cups of sliced onions
- One and 3/4 cups of all-purpose flour
- One to two cups of beef stock
- Half teaspoon Cayenne Pepper
- One and a half tablespoon salt
- One egg yolk
- Two tablespoons Cream

Instructions:

1. Melt butter in a six-quarter soup kettle, add onions, reduce the heat to very mild, and cook until the onions are melted.

2. In the first step of cooking, be careful not to tan. Add flour and simmer for an additional 5 to 10 minutes, stirring regularly. Combine with the stock, salt, and bring to a boil. Lower the flame and boil for 15 minutes or so.

3. Suspend the kettle from the heat. Whisk the egg yolk and milk together. Add a little broth and mix rapidly, and add

---

to the kettle of soup.

4. Serve in soup cups with toasted bread or croutons and scatter with buttered breadcrumbs and grated Parmesan cheese.

5. Brown under the flaming broiler and serve.

5. Gallagher's Cheddar Cheese Soup

Preparation time: 40 minutes

Servings: 8

Difficulty: Moderate

Ingredients:

- Two cups of water
- 1/3 cup finely chopped carrots
- 1/3 cup finely chopped celery
- One cup of finely chopped green onions
- Half cup butters
- A quarter cup all-purpose flour
- One cup of chopped white onion
- Four cups of milk
- Four cups of chicken broth
- 15 ounces pasteurized process cheese spread
- salt and pepper to taste
- A quarter teaspoon of Cayenne
- One tablespoon of Prepared mustard

Instructions:

1. Put water over high heat in a soup pot. Bring to a boil for 5 minutes; set aside, but do not drain. Add the carrots, celery and green onions.

2. Melt butter over medium heat in a broad stockpot and add onion; sauté for 1 minute, then add flour, mixing well.

3. Boil the milk and broth in a large saucepan. Whisk a paste of broth into a flour mixture with a wire whisk.

4. Stir in the cheese, salt, cayenne and pepper. Stir in the mustard and vegetables that have been cooked, plus the water in which they have been cooked. Bring it to a boil and immediately serve.

Chapter 3: Salad Recipes

1. Luby-Cafeteria's Green Pea Salad

Preparation time: 40 minutes

Servings: 8

Difficulty: Moderate

Ingredients:

- 32 ounces frozen green peas, thawed
- One cup of finely diced Cheddar cheese
- One cup of diced celery
- Half cup thinly sliced sweet pickle
- Half cup diced red bell pepper or pimiento
- Half cup mayonnaise
- Salt and pepper
- Lettuce leaves, for serving

Instructions:

1. Rinse the peas that are thawed and drain well. Put the remainder of the salad ingredients together and chill for 2 hours.

2. Line the lettuce leaf salad plates, top with the salad and serve.

2. California Pizza Kitchen Wedge Salad

Preparation time: 30 minutes

Servings: 2

Difficulty: Moderate

Ingredients:

- One head iceberg lettuce Blue cheese dressing, to taste
- Two peeled and chopped hard-boiled eggs
- Six slices chopped cooked bacon
- Blue cheese crumbles to taste
- Half cup chopped tomatoes

Instructions:

1. On the lettuce head, cut off any brown or dark green leaves.

2. By tapping it on a countertop, extract the inside core.

3. Cut the lettuce head in two.

4. For the lettuce wedge to lay flat, trim the opposite ends.

5. Place the blue cheese sauce on top of the lettuce.

6. Add chopped bacon and eggs.

7. Use the blue cheese crumbles and tomatoes to conclude the salad.

3. California Pizza Kitchen Waldorf Chicken Salad

Preparation time: 55 minutes

Servings: 2

Difficulty: Moderate

Ingredients:

Salad Dressing

- One cup of olive oil
- Half cup balsamic vinegar
- Two tablespoons of Dijon mustard
- One tablespoon of minced garlic
- Half teaspoon fresh ground black pepper
- 1/4 teaspoon salt

Salad

- Six cups of mixed baby greens
- Half cup diced celery
- One granny smith apple, chopped into bite-sized pieces
- Half cup halved red seedless grapes2 sliced grilled chicken breasts
- Half cup candied walnuts
- Crumbled gorgonzola cheese, to taste

Instructions:

1. In a bowl with a lid, whisk together all the dressing ingredients.

2. Before eating, cool the salad dressing and the plates in the refrigerator for 30 minutes.

3. Put together the greens, celery, and fruits and put them on the chilled plates.

4. Drizzle on the dressing for the salad.

5. Put chicken breast, candied walnuts, and gorgonzola on top of the salad.

4. Dave and Buster's Muffaletta Salad

Preparation time: 1 hour

Servings: 4

Difficulty: Moderate

Ingredients:

- 24 slices pepperoni
- Two ounces sliced salami
- Four ounces sliced ham
- Four ounces sliced turkey
- One cup of sliced celery
- Four tablespoons of chopped green onion
- One cup of roasted red peppers
- 1/4 cup sliced black olives
- Half cup chopped green salad olives
- One and 1/4 pounds spiral pasta
- Three tablespoons of Italian dressing
- One and a half cups of assorted lettuce
- 1/4 cup julienned spinach leaves
- One cup of diced Roma tomatoes
- One cup of Italian cheese blend
- 1/4 cup shredded Asiago cheese

Instructions:

1. Chop the pepperoni, salami, ham and turkey into thin strips. Put the meat in a large bowl with the salad.
2. To the dish, add the celery, green onions, and roasted peppers.
3. To the bowl, chop and add all types of olives.
4. Add the pasta that has been cooked.
5. On the pasta, pour the Italian dressing and gently toss everything together.
6. On a cold serving plate, place the assorted lettuce and spinach, leaving a space in the middle for the pasta salad.
7. Pile the mixture of the salad high in the middle of the plate.
8. Top the salad with tomatoes and cheese.

5. KFC Bean Salad

Preparation time: 25 minutes

Servings: 6

Difficulty: Moderate

Ingredients:

- One (16-ounce) can of green beans
- One (16-ounce) can of wax beans
- One (16-ounce) can of kidney beans
- One medium small-diced green pepper
- One medium small-diced white onion
- Half cup vegetable oil
- Half cup cider vinegar
- 3⁄4 cup sugar
- One and a half teaspoons of salt
- Half teaspoon black pepper

Instructions:

1. Drain and rinse all the beans.
2. Combine all the ingredients in an airtight container
3. Marinate in the refrigerator, preferably 3–4 days.
4. After the refrigeration, savor whenever you like.

Chapter 4: Main Course Recipes

1. Macaroni Grill's Scaloppine Di Pollo

Preparation time: 40 minutes

Servings: 2 to 4

Difficulty: Moderate

Ingredients:

Lemon Butter Sauce

- Four Ounces lemon juice
- Two Ounces white wine
- Four Ounces heavy cream
- One Pound butter (4 sticks)

Chicken

- Six to eight chicken breasts (3–ounces each) pounded thin
- Oil and butter for sauteing chicken
- Two and 3/4 cups of flour, seasoned with salt and pepper, for dredging
- Six Ounces pancetta, cooked
- Twelve Ounces mushrooms, sliced
- Twelve Ounces artichoke hearts, sliced
- One tablespoon of capers
- One Pound Capellini pasta, cooked

- chopped parsley for garnish

Instructions:

1. Heat the lemon juice and white wine in a saucepan over medium heat to make the sauce. Bring it to a simmer and reduce it by a third.

2. Mix in the milk and boil until the mixture thickens (3 to 4 minutes). Add butter slowly until it is fully immersed.

3. With salt and pepper, season. Remove from heat and keep warm.

4. Cook and rinse the pasta. In a large pan, melt a tiny amount of oil and two teaspoons of butter.

5. Dredge the chicken in the flour and sauté in the pan until brown and cooked through, turning once. Remove the chicken from the pan.

6. The remaining ingredients are to be added to the pan. Heat until the mushrooms are cooked and tender. Add the chicken to the pan again.

7. To serve, put on each plate, the cooked pasta. To the chicken mixture, add half of the butter sauce and toss. Taste and adjust. If needed, add more sauce.

8. Set the mixture of chicken over the pasta. To each one, add a little more sauce.

9. Use parsley to garnish.

2. The Olive Garden's Capellini Primavera

Preparation time: 45 minutes

Servings: 4 to 6

Difficulty: Moderate

Ingredients:

- Half C. (1 stick) butter
- One and a half C. chopped onions
- 3/4 C. julienne-cut carrots (1/8x1/8x1 Half -inch)
- Five C. broccoli florets, cut into 1-inch pieces
- Three C. sliced mushrooms
- One and A quarter C. thinly sliced yellow squash
- One teaspoon of minced garlic
- One and a half C. water
- One tablespoon of beef bouillon granules (or vegetable broth)
- A quarter C. sun-dried tomatoes, oil-packed, minced
- One and A quarter C. crushed tomatoes in puree
- One tablespoon of finely chopped fresh parsley
- A quarter teaspoon of dried oregano
- A quarter teaspoon of dried rosemary
- 1/8 teaspoon crushed red pepper flakes
- One lb. fresh angel-hair pasta
- Half C. grated Parmesan cheese

Instructions:

1. Over medium heat, melt the butter in a Dutch oven. Sauté the onions, carrots and

   broccoli for 5 minutes in the butter. Add the onions, garlic and squash. Sauté for two minutes.

2. Excluding pasta and cheese, add all the remaining ingredients; mix well.

3. Bring to a boil, then cook for 8-10 minutes or until soft and well blended with vegetables and flavors. Serve over cooked pasta.

4. Top with Parmesan.

3. Olive Garden Pollo Limone

Preparation time: 55 minutes

Servings: 2 to 4

Difficulty: Moderate

Ingredients:

- Four boneless skinless chicken breasts
- Three tablespoons of flour
- One and a half tablespoons olive oil
- A quarter C. finely chopped green onions
- Two minced cloves of garlic
- Half C. chicken broth
- A quarter C. dry white wine
- Two tablespoons of fresh lemon juice
- Two tablespoons of chopped fresh parsley
- One tablespoon of grated lemon peel
- salt and pepper
- One lb. chicken to A quarter-inch thick and sprinkle with salt and pepper

Instructions:

1. Set the flour in a bowl. Heat one teaspoon of oil over high heat in a nonstick skillet.

2. Cover the chicken lightly with flour and transfer to the skillet and cook until brown, for about 2 minutes per side.

3. Place the chicken on a plate and keep it warm. Heat half a teaspoon of olive oil over low heat in the same skillet.

4. Add the garlic and green onions; sauté until tender. Stir in the broth and wine, and scrape the brown bits out of the pan. Add two teaspoons of chopped parsley and lemon juice.

5. Bring to a boil and heat up to high, simmering for about 3 minutes. Mix in the lemon peel and season with salt and pepper to taste.

6. Return the chicken to the skillet and boil in the sauce until heated.

7. Place the chicken on a pan, spoon the juices over the chicken and add the remaining parsley.

4. Stouffer's Grandma's Chicken and Rice Bake

Preparation time: 1 hour 25 minutes

Servings: 2 to 4

Difficulty: Moderate

Ingredients:

- One and a half pounds boneless, skinless chicken breasts
- Three cups of instant whole grain brown rice
- Two and a half cups water or broth
- One tablespoon of olive oil, divided
- Half cup chopped onion
- Two carrots, finely diced
- One cup of frozen peas
- 18-ounce can cream of mushroom soup
- Ten and a half ounce can cream of chicken soup
- Ten and a half ounce can cheddar cheese soup
- Two cups of milk
- Eight ounces shredded cheddar or three-cheese blend
- salt and pepper
- One and a half cups Panko-style bread crumbs
- Two tablespoons of butter, melted
- Half tablespoon paprika

Instructions:

1. Preheat the oven to 350°F. Use cooking spray to spray baking dishes or disposable pans.

2. Place the chicken in a 3-quart saucepan and cover it with water. Season lightly with salt and bring to a boil, simmer over low heat and cook for 20 minutes or until the chicken is scarcely cooked (it will finish in the oven).

3. With two forks, remove chicken and dice or shred; you should have about four cups.

4. Strain and measure the liquid. To make two and a half cups, add additional water, if necessary. Place it in the same pot again and get it to a boil. Lower the heat, add the rice and cover. Cook for 5 minutes, then turn the heat off and steam for an additional 5 minutes in the covered pan until the remaining ingredients are assembled.

5. Place half the olive oil and the chicken parts in a large non-stick skillet over medium-high heat. Just stir and cook until the chicken on the edges starts to tan. Remove the chicken and set it aside. In the same skillet, put the remaining oil and the onion and carrots.

6. Cook and stir for about 4 minutes until the carrots are tender and the onion is translucent. Add the peas, then remove them from the heat.

7. Combine the three soups, the cream, and the cheese in a large bowl. Stir in the chicken, the rice, and the

vegetables gently. To taste, add salt and pepper, and spoon into prepared casseroles.

8. Stir together the bread crumbs, melted butter, then paprika and sprinkle over the casseroles evenly.

9. Bake for 40-45 minutes.

10. In the pans, let the mixture cool down completely. Wrap the plastic wrap over the whole pan and then wrap it with foil. Label and freeze.

11. Thaw in the refrigerator overnight until preparing to bake, and then bring to room temperature before unwrapping and baking as above.

5. Chili's Spicy Garlic-and-Lime Shrimp

Preparation time: 45 minutes

Servings: 4

Difficulty: Moderate

Ingredients:

Seasoning Mix

- One teaspoon of salt
- 1/4 teaspoon black pepper
- 1/4 teaspoon cayenne pepper
- 1/4 teaspoon parsley flakes
- Pinch of garlic powder
- 1/4 teaspoon paprika
- Pinch of dried thyme
- Pinch of onion powder

Shrimp

- Two tablespoons of butter
- One clove garlic, chopped
- 24 large shrimp, peeled and deveined
- One lime

Instructions:

1. Combine and set aside the ingredients for the seasoning mix.

2. In a skillet, melt the butter. Sauté 10 seconds of the garlic and add the shrimp. Over the shrimp, squeeze the lime juice and scatter with the seasoning mix.

3. Sauté for 5 to 8 minutes until the shrimp is pink and fried.

6. Claim Jumper's Pot Roast and Vegetables

Preparation time: 40 minutes

Servings: 2

Difficulty: Moderate

Ingredients:

Vegetables

- Half cup chopped carrots
- Half cup chopped turnip
- Half cup chopped sweet potato
- One medium onion, chopped
- Assorted chopped fresh herbs (thyme, rosemary, oregano)
- Olive oil
- Salt and pepper

Herb Gravy

- One clove garlic, chopped
- ¼ cup chopped shallots
- Half cup fresh herbs, chopped
- Two tablespoons of olive oil
- One cup of beef broth or store-bought au jus mix

Roast

- ounces fully cooked chuck roast, cut into 1-inch cubes
- Mashed potatoes, for serving

Instructions:

1. Preheat the oven to 375°F.

2. Roast the vegetables in a little olive oil with the fresh herbs until they are caramelized. Season with salt and pepper and leave to cool and refrigerate until ready for use in a sealed container.

3. Sauté the garlic, shallots, and fresh herbs in olive oil to make the herb gravy. Add the broth of beef and boil for 5 minutes or so; set aside.

4. Place the cubed meat with the roasted vegetables and herb gravy in a skillet and simmer just to heat it.

5. With mashed potatoes, serve.

7. Olive Garden's Risotto Milanese

Preparation time: 45 minutes

Servings: 4

Difficulty: Moderate

Ingredients:

- ¼ cup olive oil
- Half cup finely chopped onion
- Half teaspoon ground turmeric
- Half cup sliced mushrooms
- Five cups of chicken or vegetable broth
- One and a half cups of Arborio rice
- Half cup white wine
- Half cup grated Parmesan cheese
- Two tablespoons of butter
- Salt and pepper
- Fresh parsley sprigs, for garnish

Instructions:

1. Heat the olive oil over medium heat in a stockpot and sauté the onion and turmeric until the onion is tender. Add the mushrooms and sauté until some of the moisture is consumed.

2. In a saucepan, heat the broth and keep it warm.

3. Add the rice to the sautéed vegetables and stir until the olive oil mixture coats all the grains. Add the white wine and allow it to evaporate, stirring often.

4. Add the warm broth, half a cup at a time, allowing it to be absorbed, continuously stirring after each addition. Repeat this process until the rice is al dente, and all the broth is drained.

5. Remove the pan from the heat and add the Parmesan cheese and the butter. With each addition, mix gently. With salt and pepper, season.

6. Transfer and garnish with parsley in a warmed serving bowl.

8. Claim Jumper's Roasted Pork Loin

Preparation time: 35 minutes

Servings: 2

Difficulty: Moderate

Ingredients:

- One cup of chopped mixed vegetables
- One tablespoon of olive oil
- 1/4 cup salsa
- Two scoops of mashed potatoes
- 1/4 cup chopped roasted red peppers, homemade or store-bought
- One teaspoon of chopped fresh cilantro
- Half cup mixed grated Cheddar and Monterey Jack cheese
- One 6- to 7-pound cooked pork loin
- Half cup barbecue sauce
- Half cup tortilla strips
- Two biscuits

Instructions:

1 Steam the vegetables until crisp-tender, for 2 to 3 minutes. And put aside.

2 In a pan, heat the oil and add the vegetables and sauté for a couple of seconds. Add and heat the salsa, then move it to a bowl.

---

3   Put the mashed potatoes, the roasted peppers, the coriander and the blended cheeses together. With a wooden spoon or rubber spatula, blend properly.

4   For the mashed potato mixture, top up the vegetable mixture. On each of the two warmed plates, placed a bowl of the veggie-potato mix. Put alongside the bowl a serving of pork loin, glaze with a little barbecue sauce, and top with the tortilla strips.

5   At the rim of the plate, place a warm biscuit and serve immediately.

Chapter 5: Other Sides and Sauces Recipes

1. Golden Corral's Rolls

Preparation time: 50 minutes
Servings: 24 rolls
Difficulty: Moderate

Ingredients:

- On envelope (¼r teaspoons of) active dry yeast
- ¼ cup warm water (105° to 115°F)
- 1/3 cup sugar Six tablespoons of (¾ stick) unsalted butter, plus extra for the pan
- One teaspoon of salt
- One cup of hot milk
- One egg, beaten
- Four and a half cups of all-purpose flour sifted

Instructions:

1. Sprinkle the yeast over the warm water in a wide bowl and leave to proof for around 5 minutes.
2. Combine the sugar, Four tablespoons of butter, salt, and hot milk in another bowl. Until the butter is molten and the sugar is dissolved, whisk with a wooden spoon.
3. Let the mixture cool to 105 ° to 115 ° F, then apply it along the beaten egg to the proofed yeast mixture.

4. One cup at a time, add the flour, combining well after each addition. Shape the dough into a softball after the fourth cup. Sprinkle on a work surface with some of the remaining half cup flour and knead the dough for around 5 minutes, steadily focusing on all the remaining flour.

5. Oil the inside of a bowl, gently and place the dough in it, flipping it over once so that both sides are oiled. Cover it with a damp towel and set the bowl free from drafts in a warm area.

6. Punch it flat, roll it out onto a lightly floured work surface and knead for 4 to 5 minutes until the dough has doubled in size, 1 to 1 half hours. Set aside and butter an 18 by a 13-inch baking pan.

7. Tiny amounts of dough are pinched off and molded into balls. One and a half to one and 3/4 inches wide until you have 24 rolls.

8. In the prepared baking pan, position the rolls so that they do not hit one another. Cover with a damp towel and grow until doubled in bulk, 30 to 40 minutes, in a warm, draft-free place.

9. Preheat the oven to 375°F.

10. Melt two tablespoons of butter that were left. Brush the tops of the raised rolls with the melted butter using a pastry brush and bake for 18 to 20 minutes until they are browned on top.

2. Olive Garden's Gnocchi with Spicy Tomato and Wine Sauce

Preparation time: 1 hour

Servings: 8 to 12

Difficulty: Moderate

Ingredients:

- A quarter cup extra virgin olive oil
- Twelve cloves garlic, peeled
- A quarter teaspoon of red pepper flakes
- One tablespoon of chopped fresh basil, or One teaspoon of dried, plus extra for garnish
- One teaspoon of chopped fresh marjoram
- Two cups of dry white wine and two cups of chicken broth
- Two 28-ounce cans of whole tomatoes, diced tomatoes, or crushed tomatoes, with juice
- Eight tablespoons (one stick) butter, chilled, cut into pieces
- Half cup grated Parmesan cheese, plus extra for garnish
- Salt and black pepper
- Four pounds gnocchi, fresh or frozen, cooked according to the package instructions

---

Instructions:

1. In a large saucepan, heat the olive oil and sauté the garlic, red pepper flakes, one tablespoon of fresh basil and marjoram until golden brown.

2. Add the chicken broth and white wine and cook for about 10 minutes. Add the tomatoes and cook for another 30 minutes until the liquid is reduced by half.

3. Put half of it in a blender until the sauce is reduced, then puree it with the butter and half a cup of Parmesan cheese. Season with black pepper and salt.

4. With the chunky tomato mixture, return the pureed sauce to the saucepan and stir to blend.

5. In a serving bowl, place the warm gnocchi and coat it with the sauce. Use parmesan and basil to garnish.

3. Lawry's Creamed Spinach

Preparation time: 35 minutes

Servings: 8

Difficulty: Easy

Ingredients:

- 20 ounces frozen chopped spinach two packages
- Four slices of finely chopped bacon
- A quarter cup minced onion
- Four tablespoons of all-purpose flour
- Two teaspoons Lawry's seasoned salt
- One teaspoon of black pepper
- Three teaspoons of minced garlic
- Two cups of warmed milk

Instructions:

1. Cook the spinach according to the instructions given in the packet and drain well. When crisp, fried the bacon bits, set them aside. Remove most of the pan's bacon drippings.

2. Sauté the onion until very tender in the remaining pan drippings. Add bacon to the onion mixture and cook for some time.

3. It will be a thick paste roux to remove the onion/bacon mixture from the heat and stir in the flour, salt, pepper, and garlic and combine thoroughly.

4. In one step, add the warmed milk all in one. Return the mixture to medium heat, constantly stirring until smooth and thickened.

5. Add the spinach and thoroughly blend. Keep the finished dish hot until it is ready for serving.

4. Olive Garden's Italian Sausage–stuffed Portobello Mushrooms with Herbs and Parmesan Cheese

Preparation time: 45 minutes

Servings. 4

Difficulty: Moderate

Ingredients:

Cream Sauce

- Two cups of heavy cream
- A quarter cup grated Parmesan cheese
- Two tablespoons of chopped fresh basil, or two teaspoons of dried
- Salt and pepper

Stuffing

- Two large eggs
- 1/4 cup milk
- One teaspoon of chopped fresh Italian flat-leaf parsley
- One teaspoon of chopped fresh basil
- One teaspoon of chopped fresh marjoram
- One clove garlic, chopped
- One cup of finely ground garlic croutons
- A quarter cup grated Parmesan cheese
- One pound bulk Italian sausage
- Four large portobello mushrooms
- Fresh parsley sprigs or basil leaves, for garnish

Instructions:

1. Make the cream sauce first. Bring to a gentle boil the heavy cream and reduce it by half. Stir in a quarter cup of parmesan cheese, basil, salt and pepper. And put aside. Make the stuffing ready.

2. In a large bowl, whisk together the eggs, then add the milk and mix properly. Add the parsley, basil, garlic, marjoram, ground croutons, and ¼ cup of the Parmesan cheese. And put aside.

3. In a skillet, sauté the sausage, breaking it up as it cooks. Remove it with a slotted spoon until it is completely browned, then add it to the stuffing mixture, stirring well to blend.

4. Preheat the oven to 350°F.

5. Remove the stems and the mushrooms' spongy undersides so that they resemble hollowed-out bowls.

6. Place them on a baking sheet, open side down, and bake for around 8 minutes, or until they are a little soft.

7. With the sausage mixture, stuff the mushroom caps and place them back in the oven to bake for 15 to 20 minutes, until golden brown on top and cooked through.

8. Spoon some cream sauce over each mushroom for serving and garnish with a sprig of parsley or fresh basil. Serve warm.

Chapter 6: Dessert Recipes

1. Olive Garden Strawberries Romano

Preparation time: 40 minutes

Servings: 4

Difficulty: Moderate

Ingredients:

- One cup of mascarpone cheese
- 1/3 cup brown sugar
- Juice of one orange
- One tablespoon of triple sec
- One cup of whipped cream
- Two quarts quartered strawberries
- Fresh mint sprig

Instructions:

1. Combine the cheese, brown sugar, orange juice, and triple sec in a mixing bowl and blend thoroughly. Fold the whipped cream over it.

2. In a dessert dish or wine glass, place the berries. Top with a mixture of cream.

3. Garnish with a mint sprig and chill before ready to be served.

2. Outback Steakhouse Key Lime Pie

Preparation time:4 hours

Servings: 1 Pie

Difficulty: Hard

Ingredients:

Crust

- One stick butter
- One cup of graham cracker crumbs

Filling

- One cup of water
- Three cups of sugar
- One package unflavored gelatin
- One teaspoon of salt
- Juice of three limes
- One cup of condensed milk

Instructions:

1. Melt the butter in a skillet to cook the crust. Mix the crumbs in. Press it into a 9″ pie pan.

2. Heat the water, sugar, gelatin, salt, and lime juice in a pot to prepare the filling. Without boiling, add the condensed milk and heat for 5–7 minutes.

3. Into the crust, pour the filling and let the pie cool. Cool for 4 hours in the refrigerator.

3. Pizza Hut Dessert Pizza

Preparation time: 1 hour

Servings: 8

Difficulty: Moderate

Ingredients:

- One (13.8-ounce) can have refrigerated pizza dough
- One (21-ounce) can of cherry, blueberry, or apple pie filling
- Half cup flours
- Half cup brown sugar
- Half cup quick oats
- Half cup cold butter
- One teaspoon of cinnamon
- Two cups of powdered sugar
- Three tablespoons of milk
- One tablespoon of butter
- One teaspoon of vanilla

Instructions:

1. Preheat the oven to 400 degrees F.

2. On a floured board, roll the dough until it is the pizza pan's diameter. Place the dough in the pan and mold it towards the edge.

3. Brush with vegetable oil and use a fork to prick.

4. For 3 minutes, prebake the dough, then take it out of the oven.

5. Over the dough, spread the pie filling.

6. Just use a fork or pastry blender to mix the flour, brown sugar, quick oats, cold butter, and cinnamon, and spoon over the filling.

7. Place the pizza back in the oven and commence to bake for 10-15 minutes or until a golden brown is in the crust. Afterward, remove from the oven.

8. By combining powdered sugar, milk, butter, and vanilla, create the vanilla drizzle. Pour the glaze over the pizza.

4. Starbucks Black Bottom Cupcakes

Preparation time: 45 minutes

Servings: 36 cupcakes

Difficulty: Moderate

Ingredients:

- One (8-ounce) package softened cream cheese
- 1/3 cup sugar
- One large egg
- Pinch salt
- Two cups of semisweet mini chocolate chips
- Three cups of flour
- Two cups of sugar
- 2/3 cup sifted unsweetened baking cocoa
- Two teaspoons of baking soda
- Half teaspoon salt
- Two cups of water
- 2/3 cup oil
- Two tablespoons of white vinegar
- Three teaspoons of vanilla

Instructions:

1. Preheat the oven to 350°F. Line 36 muffin tins of standard size with paper liners.

2. Beat the cream cheese, sugar, egg, and salt in a bowl until they are soft and well mixed. To blend, put in the chocolate chips and mix. And put aside.

3. Sift flour, sugar, cocoa, baking soda, and salt together in a bowl.

4. Whisk the water, oil, vinegar, and vanilla together in a small bowl. Beat well until mixed thoroughly.

5. Combine the wet and then dry ingredients.

6. Fill 3/4 of the liners with chocolate batter and drop about one teaspoon of the cream cheese mixture on top of each chocolate batter and in the middle.

7. Bake for about 20 minutes or until the test for the cupcakes is done.

5. Starbucks Oatmeal Cookies

Preparation time: 50 minutes
Servings: 36 cookies
Difficulty: Moderate

Ingredients:

- One and a half cups of old-fashioned oats
- Half cup flour
- 1/4 cup dark raisins
- 1/4 cup golden raisins
- 1/4 cup dried cranberries
- 1/4 teaspoon baking powder
- 1/4 teaspoon baking soda
- Half teaspoon salt
- Six tablespoons of room-temperature butter
- Half cup packed dark brown sugar
- 1/4 cup sugar
- One large egg
- Half teaspoon ground cinnamon
- One teaspoon of vanilla
- Four tablespoons of dark raisins for topping
- Four tablespoons of golden raisins for topping

Instructions:

1. Preheat the oven to 350 degrees F
2. Oats, flour, raisins, cranberries, baking powder, baking soda, and salt are mixed. And put aside.
3. Whisk together the butter and sugar until light and fluffy. Add the egg, vanilla, and cinnamon and beat until blended.
4. Add the oat mixture to the butter mixture steadily. Beat before they're mixed.
5. In a different bowl, blend and set aside the raisins for the topping.
6. Drop the dough onto two thinly greased baking sheets with rounded tablespoons, 2″ apart.
7. On top of the dough, place one rounded teaspoon of raisins.
8. Bake until the cookies are golden brown but still soft, around 12-16 minutes.
9. Cool on sheets before serving.

6. Subway White Chocolate Macadamia Nut Cookies

Preparation time: 50 minutes

Servings: 24 Cookies

Difficulty: Moderate

Ingredients:

- Half cup butter
- 3⁄4 cup sugar
- One egg
- One teaspoon of vanilla extract
- One and 1⁄4 cups of flour
- Half teaspoon baking soda
- Half teaspoon salt
- Eight ounces chopped white chocolate
- One (6.5-ounce) jar of chopped macadamia nuts

Instructions:

1. Preheat the oven to 375°F.
2. Cream the butter and the sugar together in a medium bowl. Stir in the vanilla and egg.
3. Stir in the creamed mixture and combine the flour, baking soda, and salt.
4. Stir in the nuts and chocolate.
5. Drop the cookies, approximately 2″ apart, by heaping teaspoonfuls on an ungreased cookie sheet.
6. Bake until lightly browned, for 8-10 minutes.

7. On wire racks, let it cool. When cool, store it in an airtight container.

7. Taco Bell Caramel Apple Empanadas

Preparation time: 45 minutes

Servings: 12

Difficulty: Moderate

Ingredients:

- One (12-ounce) package of Stouffer's frozen harvest apples
- One tablespoon of flour
- 1/4 cup butter
- 1/4 cup firmly packed light brown sugar
- 1/4 teaspoon ground allspice
- Three and a half cups of baking mix
- One cup of whipping cream
- Two tablespoons of melted butter

Instructions:

1. Preheat the oven to 400 degrees F.
2. Thaw the apples for 6–7 minutes at half power in the microwave. For 3 minutes, make them stand. With the flour, stir together.
3. Melt half a cup of butter over medium heat in a medium skillet. Add the mixture of apples, brown sugar and allspice. Cook, constantly stirring, for 4 minutes or until the mixture thickens. Suspend from the heat.
4. Mash the apple mixture coarsely and set aside.

5. Stir together the baking mix and whisk the cream until moistened with a fork. On a well-floured surface, turn out the dough and knead 3-4 times.

6. Roll the dough to a thickness of ½" and cut it into 12 squares (5").

7. Divide the apple mixture into 12 servings and in the middle of each square, place one serving.

8. Fold over the square on one side, pressing the edges with a fork to secure. Place on a baking sheet that is lightly oiled. With melted butter, brush the tops and bake for 18-20 minutes or golden brown.

8. The Melting Pot Dark Chocolate Raspberry Fondue

Preparation time: 35 minutes

Servings: 2 to 4

Difficulty: Moderate

Ingredients:

- ounces finely chopped dark chocolate

- 1/4 cup heavy cream

- Three tablespoons of raspberry liqueur

Instructions:

1. In a microwave-safe bowl, combine the chocolate and cream.

2. Heat for 2–3 minutes in the microwave on medium heat, stopping to stir after 30 seconds. Better take note not to make the chocolate burn.

3. Pour into a pot of warm crock or fondue.

4. Drizzle the liqueur with it. Suggested dippers contain graham crackers, marshmallows, and fruit.

9. The Melting Pot Flaming Turtle Fondue

Preparation time: 35 minutes

Servings: 2 to 4

Difficulty: Moderate

Ingredients:

- Two ounces melted milk chocolate

- Two ounces caramel sundae syrup

- Whole milk for thinning, if necessary

- 1/3 ounce of 151 rum

- One ounce of chopped pecans

Instructions:

1. In a saucepan, heat the chocolate and caramel over low heat, stirring regularly.

2. If the mixture is too thick, add the whole milk slowly to achieve the best consistency.

3. Add the rum to the pot slowly.

4. By touching the flame to the pot's edge, carefully ignite the liquor using a long match.

5. Add the nuts to the pot and mix until the flame burns out.

10. Waldorf Astoria Red Velvet Cake

Preparation time: 1 hour

Servings: 16

Difficulty: Moderate

Ingredients:

Cake

- Half cup shortening
- Two eggs
- Two ounces red food coloring
- One cup of buttermilk
- One tablespoon of vinegar
- One teaspoon of baking soda
- One and a half cups sugar
- Three tablespoons of cocoa
- Two and A quarter cups of all-purpose flour
- 3/4 teaspoon salt
- One teaspoon of vanilla

Frosting

- Three tablespoons of all-purpose flour
- One cup of milk
- Half cup shortening
- Half cup butter
- One cup of sugar
- One teaspoon of vanilla

Instructions:

1. Preheat the oven to 350°F.

2. Take three cake pans and dust with oil and flour.

3. Create cocoa and food coloring paste.

4. In a bowl with cream shortening, eggs, and sugar, add the mix of cocoa and food coloring. Mix thoroughly.

5. Add buttermilk with vinegar and flour with salt alternately.

6. Fold in vanilla with baking soda by hand.

7. Pour batter into cake pans in similar proportions.

8. Bake at 350 F for 30 minutes or until it comes out clean with a toothpick inserted in the middle.

9. Remove the layers of cake from the pans and let it cool.

10. Cook the flour and milk until thick to make the frosting.

11. Beat shortening, sugar, margarine, vanilla until smooth.

12. Add the combination of milk and flour a little at a time and stir well.

13. Pour it over the cake, let cool and serve.

Chapter 7: Beverages Recipes

1. Outback Steakhouse Wallaby Darned

Preparation time: 25 minutes

Servings: 2

Difficulty: Easy

Ingredients:

- Eight ounces of frozen sliced peaches

- Half cup Bacardi Fuzzy Navel mix

- Half cup ice

- Half cup champagne

- Three ounces of water

- One and a half ounces peach schnapps

- One and a half ounces vodka

- One tablespoon of sugar

Instructions:

1. Place all the drink ingredients into a blender.

2. Blend until smooth.

3. Pour into 2 (10-ounce) glasses and serve immediately.

2. T.G.I. Friday's Chocolate Monkey

Preparation time: 25 minutes

Servings: 1

Difficulty: Easy

Ingredients:

- Half ripe banana

- Two scoops of vanilla ice cream

- One scoop of crushed ice

- One ounce banana liqueur

- Half ounce chocolate syrup

- Whipped cream for garnish

- Banana slices, for garnish

- Cherry, for garnish

Instructions:

1. Place all the drink ingredients into a blender. Blend until thick and creamy.

2. Serve in a tall wine glass with a straw. Top with whipped cream.

3. Garnish with banana slices and a cherry.

3. T.G.I. Friday's Flying Grasshopper

Preparation time: 25 minutes

Servings: 1

Difficulty: Easy

Ingredients:

- 3⁄4 ounce of green Crème de Menthe

- 3⁄4 ounce of white Crème de Cacao

- 3⁄4 ounce of vodka

- Two scoops of vanilla ice cream

- Half scoop crushed ice

Instructions:

1. Combine all the ingredients in a blender. Blend until smooth.

2. Serve in tall specialty glass.

4. Tommy Bahama Millionaire Mojito

Preparation time: 15 minutes

Servings: 1

Difficulty: Easy

Ingredients:

- Two parts Tommy Bahama White Sand Rum

- One teaspoon of superfine sugar

- Juice of one lime

- Crushed ice

- Dash of sparkling soda

- One bunch of fresh mint

Instructions:

1. In a shaker, mix the rum, sugar, and lime juice. Add ice.

2. Shake well and pour into a glass that is chilled.

3. Add sparkling soda.

4. Garnish with a sprig of mint.

Conclusion

I'm very glad you've taken the time to read this book.

I hope that with regards to Copycat Recipes, all your questions are clear.

It is about learning the restaurants' simple ingredients and techniques to make the masterpiece dish to create a Copycat Recipe.

Creating a copy of the popular restaurant dish also allows you to adjust the ingredients used according to your tastes and health restrictions to produce a custom recipe.

It is also a cost-effective way to eat popular meals that you want.

Keep cooking and try to work with the recipes.

Well, thanks and good luck!

CPSIA information can be obtained
at www.ICGtesting.com
Printed in the USA
BVHW061016220321
603175BV00003B/176

9 781914 129612